Do You KNOW?™

THE CIVIL WAR

A brain-stretching quiz about the historic
struggle between the blue and gray

Guy Robinson

S0-ALH-757

SOURCEBOOKS, INC.®
NAPERVILLE, ILLINOIS

Published by Sourcebooks, Inc.
P.O. Box 4410, Naperville, Illinois 60567-4410
(630) 961-3900
Fax: (630) 961-2168
www.sourcebooks.com

ISBN-13: 978-1-4022-1297-0
ISBN-10: 1-4022-1297-6

Printed and bound in the United States of America
SP 10 9 8 7 6 5 4 3 2

The War Between the States, as well as the time leading to the conflict and the period of rebuilding that followed, strained the population and ruptured the nation in ways that have been felt for a century and a half. Little wonder, then, that so many people devour the details of the era: the politicians and their moves, the military leaders and their strengths and failings, the battles, the spies, the songs, the Civil War movies of our own time, facts and factlets of all sorts.

Which is where this little quiz comes in. It's by no means a complete exam on everything to do with the Civil War period. But because the questions range over a wide variety of categories, this test should give you a good opportunity to show what you know—and what you don't. There are some easy scores to be had among the questions here, but others may make you scratch your head or send you hunting through the history books.

So here are 100 questions. Count ten points for each correct answer. Where a question has more than one part, you'll be told how to divide the credit. Here and there you'll find a chance to earn five or ten bonus points, so it's theoretically possible to score more than 1,000. (But you won't!)

Figure your performance this way:

Above 900:	**Spectacular!**
700–899:	A very solid showing
500–699:	Nothing to be ashamed of
Below 500:	Told you it was tough

1. The full title of Harriet Beecher Stowe's 1852 anti-slavery book, the best-selling novel of the 19th century, was *Uncle Tom's Cabin, or...*

    a. *A Tale of Slaves*
    b. *Life Among the Lowly*
    c. *On and Off the Mighty Mississipp'*
    d. *How It Really Was*

2. In 1856, on the floor of the U.S. Senate, during arguments about slavery, a South Carolina congressman clubbed a Massachusetts senator on the head with a cane. Name either politician. (Ten extra points if you can name both.)

3. Which chief justice wrote the 1857 landmark U.S. Supreme Court decision in *Dred Scott v. Sandford*?

    a. Oliver Ellsworth
    b. John Marshall
    c. Roger B. Taney
    d. Salmon P. Chase

4. What were "Beecher's Bibles"?

5. When the anti-slavery guerrilla leader John Brown raided the federal arsenal at Harper's Ferry in 1859, looking for weapons to use for a slave uprising, about how many men joined him in the assault?

    a. More than 100
    b. 30 to 40
    c. 15 to 20
    d. He was alone

6. When he was running for president in 1860, Abraham Lincoln was called—among other things—"Old Abe." Within two years, how old was he at the time?

7. To which church did Lincoln belong?

    a. Presbyterian
    b. Episcopal

    c. Unitarian
    d. None

8. Before Lincoln's inauguration, in March 1861, seven states seceded from the Union. South Carolina was first. Which state was second? (Ten bonus points for naming the other five.)

_____

9. Richmond wasn't the first capital of the Confederate States of America. For five points, which city was first, and for five more, how long did it host the new government?

_____

10. Abe Lincoln and Jefferson Davis had some things in common—three of these four, in fact. Which statement *isn't* true?

    a. They were born in the same state
    b. They assumed the presidency at the same age
    c. Each suffered the death of a young son while in office
    d. Each studied at West Point

11. Lincoln's vice president during his first term was Hannibal Hamlin, of the state of: _____

12. Alexander Hamilton Stephens, vice president of the C.S.A., came to the job after deep involvement in secession discussions in his home state of Georgia. How did he stand on the question of leaving to form a new nation?

    a. Strongly in favor
    b. In favor with qualifications

    c. Opposed
    d. Abstained

13. Under President James Buchanan, I was attorney general. Under Lincoln, I held a different cabinet post. During the war, I favored arming freed slaves so that they could fight the enemy. I was the guy who, just after Lincoln died, said, "Now he belongs to the ages" (or, as some would have it, "Now he belongs to the angels"), yet later some gossips thought I might have been involved in the assassination plot. Who was I?

_____

14. Allan Pinkerton, who founded his own detective outfit in Chicago, served as head of a government spy agency charged with guarding the president. In 1861, he and his agents foiled what was called a plot to assassinate Lincoln on the way to his inauguration. What was that early agency called?

    a. Union Intelligence Service
    b. Central Espionage Bureau
    c. National Bureau of Secret and Preventive Maneuvers
    d. Homeland Protection Agency

15. The Civil War's first shots were heard on April 12, 1861, when Confederate soldiers fired on Fort Sumter, a federal facility in Charleston Harbor held by Union troops. The general outside the fort had studied artillery at West Point under the leader of the soldiers inside. Ten points for the name of either man, and ten extra points for the other.

_____

16. When it was clear that a war was underway, Lincoln called for volunteers to fight the Southerners. At that stage, for how long were men expected to sign up?

    a. Three months   c. Twenty-four months
    b. Twelve months   d. Thirty-six months

17. After the outbreak of war, the U.S. Navy burned and sank a wooden frigate, the *Merrimac*, at Norfolk, to keep it out of Confederate hands. The Confederate Navy raised the hulk, converted it into an ironclad ship, and re-christened it. With what name? (For ten extra points, what Union ship did it face in the first-ever battle of ironclad warships?)

    a. Alabama   c. Dixie
    b. Norfolk   d. Virginia

18. Early in the war, Lincoln negotiated with a European hero who offered his services to the Union but added some requirements (such as a promise to abolish slavery) that the president declined to meet. Who was it who, in the end, didn't help?

_____

19. Who led the Union military at the start of the war, until he was replaced, in November 1861, by General George B. McClellan?

_____

20. What was the name given to antiwar Northern Democrats? (For ten bonus points, what Ohioan was the most prominent member of the faction?)

_____

21. What former explorer and anti-slavery candidate for president, while commander of the Union Army's Department of the West, issued a unilateral emancipation proclamation for slaves of Missouri? (Lincoln, waiting for the right time to issue his own proclamation, voided the order.)

_____

22. Levi Coffin, the North Carolina-born abolitionist who played a major role shepherding slaves to freedom in Canada through the Underground Railroad, operated chiefly in which one of these states? (For ten bonus points, in which of them did William Still, a northern son of ex-slaves, play a leading part in Railroad operations?)

a. Ohio

b. Indiana

c. Pennsylvania

d. New York

23. Civil War flicks? It's not just *Gone with the Wind*. For two points each, identify these notable Civil War movies:

a. Audie Murphy stars in John Huston's take on the Stephen Crane classic ('51): _____

b. Matthew Broderick and Denzel Washington with a very special Union regiment ('89): _____

c. Buster Keaton silent classic about a train engineer, the Southern cause, and love ('27): _____

d. Super-long screen version of *The Killer Angels*, partly filmed on the battlefield ('93): _____

e. Elvis, in his movie debut, marries his brother's gal—and sings the title song ('56): _____

24. Who was pushed out as governor of the newly seceded state of Texas after he refused to profess loyalty to the Confederacy?

_____

25. For two points each, match the Civil War figure with the nickname:

a. "The Rock of Chickamauga"

b. "Old Reliable"

c. "Unconditional Surrender"

d. "The Gray Ghost"

e. "Blast"

f. Ulysses S. Grant

g. John Bratton

h. Benjamin F. Butler

i. George H. Thomas

j. James Ewell Brown (Jeb) Stuart

26. What was the name of the British steamship that was at the center of a tense standoff between the Union and Great Britain in 1861?

_____

27. During the course of his career, Robert E. Lee went by several nicknames. In fact, at one time or another he was called all but just one of these. Which?

    a. "Uncle Robert"   d. "Ace of Spades"
    b. "Marse Robert"   e. "Granny"
    c. "Rapid Robert"

28. In 1862, thanks to the stress of the war on the Union treasury, the country saw its first income tax—a simple flat tax. Within months, a two-bracket structure first took over, but what was the percentage when that first, supremely simple tax went into effect?

    a. 2% on net income above $600
    b. 3% on net income above $800
    c. 3½ % on net income above $2,500
    d. 4% on net income above $500
    e. 5% on net income above $1,000

29. Which ex-president of the U.S.A. died in 1862 but was not officially mourned in Washington because he had supported the Confederacy?

_____

30. Confederate leaders Robert E. Lee and P.G.T. Beauregard each took over in battle upon the wounding—and in one case the subsequent death—of a different commander named Johnston. For five points each, name the two Johnstons involved, and explain the circumstances.

    Lee's Johnston: _____

    Beauregard's Johnston: _____

31. Belle Boyd, the Confederate spy, carried out her espionage activities throughout the war without once being caught. True or false?

_____

32. What was the real name of the Union spy known as "Crazy Bet," whose cover included walking the streets of Richmond, talking to herself?

_____

33. The name Seven Days Battles refers to a series of encounters—at Beaver Dam Creek, Gaines' Mill, Savage's Station, White Oak Swamp, Glendale, and Malvern Hill—in which General Lee faced the invading Union Army of the Potomac outside Richmond in the early summer of 1862, with heavy casualties on both sides. Which Union major general opposed Lee throughout those battles?

    a. Ambrose E. Burnside   c. George B. McClellan
    b. Joseph Hooker   d. George G. Meade

34. Robert E. Lee's wife was the great-granddaughter of:

    a. Martha Washington   c. Sophia Dorothea of Hanover
    b. Abigail Adams   d. Marie Antoinette

35. George Todd, brother of Mary Todd Lincoln, the president's wife, was a surgeon in the Confederate Army. And that's not all: Which of these other relatives of Mrs. Lincoln served the Confederacy?

    a. Her half-brother, David Todd
    b. Her half-brother, Samuel Todd
    c. Her half-brother, Alexander Todd
    d. Her half-sister's husband, Benjamin Hardin Helm

36. **Which one of these songs of the era did Confederacy sympathizers favor?**

    a. "When Johnny Comes Marching Home"
    b. "Marching Through Georgia"
    c. "John Brown's Body"
    d. "Tramp! Tramp! Tramp!"
    e. "For Bales"

37. **A copy of General Lee's plan to invade Maryland was lost in the field and retrieved by a Union soldier, who found it wrapped around three cigars in an envelope. What was the official order number of that document?**

    a. 11   c. 119
    b. 19   d. 191

38. **Robert E. Lee's most famous horse was Traveller, appropriately gray in color and with Lee throughout his wartime service and behind the casket in his funeral procession in 1870. Here are five other well-known Civil War horses. For two points each, match them with the military men who rode them:**

    a. Baldy   f. George G. Meade
    b. Cincinnati   g. Ulysses S. Grant
    c. Kentucky   h. Stonewall Jackson
    d. Lexington   i. William T. Sherman
    e. Little Sorrel   j. George B. McClellan

39. **Which end-of-statement is true? At West Point, Robert E. Lee…**

    a. …finished second in the class of 1829
    b. …failed a senior seminar on History of Military Tactics
    c. …was suspended for a week for discharging a weapon in chapel
    d. …roomed with three cadets, all of whom later became Union generals

40. "So this is the little woman who made this big war." To whom did Lincoln reportedly say that when they met?

_____

41. What important American poet searched the front lines in Virginia for his wounded soldier brother, and later volunteered as a nurse in and around Washington, DC?

_____

42. How did Stonewall Jackson die?

   a. Shot in a poker game
   b. Fell from a horse
   c. Accidentally shot by one of his own men during the war
   d. Poisoned by unclean drinking water

43. Where did General Grant fight and win the six-week-long battle for the fort that gave the Union control of the Mississippi River, effectively splitting the Confederacy in two?

_____

44. The 37th Iowa Volunteer Infantry Regiment consisted of men beyond draft age, 45. What was the unit's nickname?

   a. "The Old Timers"   c. "The Tried and True"
   b. "The Graybeard Regiment"   d. "The Swell Seniors"

45. In his pre-Confederacy days as war secretary under President Franklin Pierce, Jefferson Davis organized an experiment in military transportation for the U.S. Army in the Southwest. What kind of transport did the trial use?

   a. Hot air balloons   c. Ostriches
   b. Foot-powered railroad cars d. Camels

46. How many days did the Battle of Gettysburg last?

a. 1
b. 2
c. 3
d. 7
e. 14

47. When the Union Army began to form fighting units of African-American men in 1863, the War Department established the:

a. Division of Negro Troops (DNT)
b. Bureau of Colored Troops (BCT)
c. Department of African-American Troops (DAAT)
d. Black Soldiers' Branch (BSB)

48. Thomas Nast, Winslow Homer, Frederic Remington—which artist *didn't* contribute battle sketches to *Harper's Weekly* during the Civil War?

_____

49. Which locale *isn't* associated with the Battle of Gettysburg?

a. Culp's Hill
b. Cemetery Ridge
c. Champion Hill
d. Little Round Top
e. Seminary Ridge
f. Devil's Den
g. Wheatfield
h. Peach Orchard

50. The biggest Confederate military prison was in:

_____

51. In 1863, fleets of which country paid supportive visits to New York and San Francisco, indicating to France and Britain that they would be wise to keep out of the American Civil War?

_____

52. In the North, the military draft aroused an opposition that set off significant mob riots in:

a. Boston

c. New York

b. Chicago

d. Hartford

53. Who led the guerrilla band that murdered, looted, and burned its way through the pro-Union settlement in Lawrence, Kansas?

_____

54. Both Union and Confederacy began the war with volunteers, but after a year the Confederates instituted a draft, and less than another year later the Union did the same. Under the terms of the Union conscription law, by paying a set fee a Northerner could escape service. How much?

a. $300

c. $1000

b. $995

d. $5,000

55. Three of these statements about photographer Matthew Brady are true. Which one *isn't?*

a. Before the Civil War, he was a New York commercial photographer, portraits a specialty

b. Most of the war photos with his credit line were actually shot by others on his team

c. Shot in the chest in battle, he was unharmed thanks to a photographic plate in his pocket

d. His ambitious war enterprise ultimately bankrupted him

56. What's the claim to fame of the Confederate vessel the *H.L. Hunley?*

_____

57. For two points each, match the Civil War figure with the quote attributed to him:

a. "With all my devotion to the Union and the feeling of loyalty and duty of an American citizen, I have not been able to raise my hand against my relatives, my children, my home."

b. "I propose to fight it out on this line if it takes all summer."

c. "All we ask is to be let alone."

d. "Damn the torpedoes!"

e. "War is cruelty. There is no use trying to reform it. The crueler it is, the sooner it will be over."

f. Jefferson Davis
g. David Farragut
h. William T. Sherman
i. Robert E. Lee
j. Ulysses S. Grant

58. Five more quotes:

a. "May God have mercy on General Lee, for I will have none."

b. "Charge the enemy and remember old Virginia!"

c. "Hold the fort—I am coming!"

d. "It is well that war is so terrible— we should grow too fond of it."

e. "They couldn't hit an elephant at this distance."

f. Robert E. Lee
g. John Sedgwick
h. Joseph Hooker
i. William T. Sherman
j. George Pickett

59. And which one of these lines is *not* attributed to Lincoln?

a. "I believe that this government cannot endure permanently half slave and half free."

b. "If we do not make common cause to save the good old ship of the Union on this voyage, nobody will have a chance to pilot her on another voyage."

c. "I claim not to have controlled events, but confess plainly that events have controlled me."

d. "As I would not be a slave, so I would not be a master."

e. "I believe it to be the duty of everyone to unite in the restoration of the country and the reestablishment of peace and harmony."

60. What Union commander handed out bronze decorations to men who tried to retake Fort Sumter in the summer of 1863?

_____

61. For two points each, match the Civil War leader to his middle name. (Five extra points for giving Robert E. Lee's middle name.)

   a. George McClellan
   b. William Sherman
   c. Edwin Stanton
   d. Simon Buckner
   e. George Meade

   f. McMasters
   g. Bolivar
   h. Brinton
   i. Gordon
   j. Tecumseh

62. What politician served under President Lincoln as U.S. minister to Russia, where he witnessed Alexander II's emancipation of the serfs in 1861, prompting him to push Lincoln to do likewise?

_____

63. After a failed raid on Richmond, papers were found on the body of the Union colonel in charge of the foray, Ulric Dahlgren. The papers, whose authenticity is still questioned, outlined a plot to...

   a. ...break into the Confederate Treasury
   b. ...kill President Davis and his cabinet
   c. ...kidnap General Lee
   d. ...kidnap John Wilkes Booth

64. During the Gettysburg Campaign, who led the division that briefly occupied York, Pennsylvania, the largest Northern town to fall during the war? (For ten bonus points, how long was York occupied?)

_____

65. Ten points for naming any two of Robert E. Lee's three sons, and ten more for the third. (All were military.)

_____

_____

_____

66. At the battlefield cemetery dedication ceremony at Gettysburg, on November 19, 1863, the featured speaker was, of course, not President Lincoln. It was Edward Everett, the Massachusetts orator. Lincoln's talk lasted less than three minutes. How long did Everett's take?

a. Half an hour

b. An hour

c. An hour and a half

d. Two hours

67. General Ulysses S. Grant said that for the rest of his life he regretted an 1864 encounter in Virginia, the Battle of:

_____

68. What Union general was targeted by war reporters, who conspired to mention his name in their stories only in connection with bad news, giving credit for wins to Grant?

_____

69. Who was called "The Brains of the Confederacy"?

_____

70. The men named in the answers to the two previous questions were both born outside the United States. For five points each, where?

The general: _____

"The Brains": _____

71. The original flag of the Confederacy was the red-white-and-blue "Stars and Bars," not the better-known, later flag with a large cross. The number of stars changed as more states seceded. The number of stripes stayed constant. How many stripes were there?

    a. 3
    b. 6
    c. 11
    d. 13

72. "Forget it, Louis. No Civil War picture ever made a nickel." Who was supposed to have said that, to whom, about what?

_____

73. What happened to Lincoln's secretary of the treasury after he resigned in 1864?

_____

74. Buffalo Bill Cody and Wild Bill Hickok both saw action during the war. On which side?

Cody: _____

Hickok: _____

75. After 22 months at sea seizing Union merchant vessels, the Confederate raider *Alabama* was finally done in by the *U.S.S. Kearsarge*. Where was the fatal battle? (Five bonus points each for the names of the captains.)

    a. Off Charleston, South Carolina
    b. In New York Harbor
    c. In Mobile Bay
    d. Off Cherbourg, France

76. The important Gulf port taken for the North by Admiral Farragut in August 1864:

_____

77. The Union military leader who was the Democrats' nominee for president in 1864, losing to Lincoln:

a. George B. McClellan
b. Ulysses S. Grant
c. Philip H. Sheridan
d. George Armstrong Custer

78. Civil War song about a "maid with golden hair" (the tune was fitted with new lyrics to become "Love Me Tender"):

_____

79. The fire that devastated Atlanta began at a:

a. Sawmill
b. Paper warehouse
c. Gas works
d Church

80. Which Union soldier rose to brevet major general at age 20, the youngest ever to hit any rank of general?

_____

81. How long was Sherman's March to the Sea, the scorched-earth drive that followed the taking of Atlanta?

a. 99 miles
b. 150 miles
c. 300 miles
d. 666 miles

82. In November 1864, a late-in-the-war Confederate plan called for agents to burn which northern city? (The plan fizzled.)

a. Boston
b. Chicago
c. New York
d. Hartford

83. Which Confederate general wore a scarlet-lined cape and an ostrich plume in his hat?

_____

84. Who yelled "Chickamauga, Chickamauga!" as they charged at Missionary Ridge, in Chattanooga? Was it Union or Rebel troops?

_____

85. The best-remembered couplet from "Barbara Frietchie," John Greenleaf Whittier's poetic account of a fictional incident during the Civil War, is the line Ms. Frietchie shouts at the soldiers marching past her house:

> *"Shoot, if you must, this old gray head,*
> *But spare your country's flag," she said.*

And what does the blushing leader call out to his troops?

_____

_____

86. General Ulysses S. Grant was known to be a decent artist. His favorite subject:

   a. Children   c. Horses

   b. Flags   d. Fruit

87. Put these five Civil War battles in chronological order, starting with the earliest.

   a. Battle of Stones River   d. Battle of the Wilderness

   b. Battle of Chancellorsville   e. First Battle of Bull Run

   c. Battle of New Orleans

88. What number did President Lincoln ask the band to play for the crowd that gathered at the White House after Lee's surrender, saying that the Union armies had "fairly captured" the song?

   a. "Dixie"

   b. "Battle Hymn of the Republic"

   c. "I've Been Working on the Railroad"

   d. "Maryland, My Maryland"

89. Here are four statements about the meeting at Appomattox Court House, Virginia, where General Lee surrendered to General Grant on April 9, 1865. Just one statement is true. Which?

    a. Grant and Lee didn't speak a word to each other
    b. Grant and Lee ate a long lunch, with plentiful wine, before discussing surrender terms
    c. Grant agreed to let Rebel soldiers take their horses home with them
    d. Lee asked for a prayer break every ten minutes

90. On April 14, 1865, four years after Union troops turned Fort Sumter over to the Confederacy, what ceremonial flourish at the fort signaled that the U.S.A. was back?

    _____

91. Ten points for naming either of the two people who were in the presidential box at Ford's Theatre with the Lincolns the night the president was shot. (And ten bonus points if you name them both.)

    _____

92. John Wilkes Booth fired his Derringer during a big laugh line in Act III, Scene 2, of *Our American Cousin*. Which of these finishes the line: "Well, I guess I know enough to turn you inside out, you…"

    a. "…scalawag"
    b. "…round-faced gatherer of mushrooms"
    c. "…sockdologizing old man trap"
    d. "…Yankee loser"

93. Booth was tracked out of Washington and trapped:

    a. in a tobacco barn in Virginia
    b. near the battlefield at Gettysburg
    c. in another theater in Washington
    d. at a schoolbook depository in Texas

94. More than a month after Lee's surrender, when hostilities were by general agreement over, a Union force attacked a small Confederate camp in Texas—on two consecutive days. Both times, the Confederates pushed the attackers back. Name that battle, the last real battle of the Civil War.

_____

95. The paddle wheeler chugged up the Mississippi, groaning and straining under the stress of its far-over-the-limit load of passengers—most of them former POWs returning home after release from Confederate prison compounds. North of Memphis, a boiler exploded and the vessel burned and sank, taking perhaps 1,700 passengers with it. The name of the steamboat?

_____

96. Five more Civil War movies. Two points for each title:

   a. Fess Parker (Fess Parker!) as a Union spy in an adventure tale that stays on track ('56): _____

   b. Pacifist Quaker Hoosiers watch and worry as the Civil War comes to town ('56): _____

   c. Clark Gable down on the plantation, with Yvonne De Carlo and Sidney Poitier ('57): _____

   d. James Stewart as a Virginian farmer and father who can't help but get involved ('65): _____

   e. The Civil War and its aftermath—a history lesson from the KKK point of view ('15): _____

97. For the former Confederate states, readmission to the Union called for some hoop jumping, and that took time. For five points each, which state was first to rejoin the fold and have elected senators and representatives back in the U.S. Congress, and which was last?

First: _____

Last: _____

98. According to the book, what was Scarlett O'Hara's real first name?

_____

99. Who was John Frederick Parker, and what *didn't* he do?

_____

100. For two points each:

   a. Which amendment to the U.S. Constitution ended slavery?
   b. Which state was first to ratify it?
   c. Which state's ratification finalized it?
   d. Which was the last state to ratify the amendment?
   e. When it took effect, which two states still allowed slavery?

ANSWERS

1. b.

2. Preston Brooks was the clubber, Charles Sumner the clubee

3. c.

4. Rifles surreptitiously shipped by the rabidly abolitionist clergyman Henry Ward Beecher to groups opposing pro-slavery forces in the Kansas Territory in the 1850s; the weapons were packed in crates labeled "BIBLES"

5. c.

6. 51

7. d.

8. Mississippi (bonus: Florida, Alabama, Georgia, Louisiana, Texas)

9. Montgomery, Alabama; under four months

10. Only d. is untrue (Davis was a West Pointer, Lincoln wasn't); a. (Kentucky), b. (52), and c. (Willie Lincoln, at 11; and Joe Davis, at 5) are correct

11. Maine

12. c.

13. Edwin Stanton (secretary of war)

14. a.

15. Brigadier General P.G.T. Beauregard, of the Confederate forces, and his former teacher, Major Robert Anderson, in command of Fort Sumter

16. a.

17. d. (extra points: the *Monitor*, which dueled the *Virginia* to a draw)

18. The Italian military man, Giuseppe Garibaldi

19. The septuagenarian General Winfield Scott

20. Copperheads (bonus: Clement L. Vallandigham)

21. John C. Frémont

22. b. (bonus: c.)

23. a. *The Red Badge of Courage*, b. *Glory*, c. *The General*, d. *Gettysburg*, e. *Love Me Tender*

24. Sam Houston

25. a.-i., b.-g., c.-f., d.-j., e.-h.

26. *Trent*

27. c.

28. b.

29. President No. 10, John Tyler

30. Lee replaced General Joseph Eggleston Johnston after Johnston was wounded at the Battle of Seven Pines; Beauregard replaced General Albert Sidney Johnston after that Johnston bled to death from a leg wound in the Battle of Shiloh

31. False—she was nabbed more than once but never put out of business for long

32. Elizabeth Van Lew

33. c.

34. a. (by Martha's first husband)

35. All of them; David was wounded in action and the other three were killed fighting for the Confederacy

36. e.

37. d.

38. a.-f., b.-g., c.-j., d.-i., e.-h.

39. a.

40. Harriet Beecher Stowe, whose book *Uncle Tom's Cabin* had greatly contributed to polarizing the nation over the issue of slavery

41. Walt Whitman

42. c. (returning from a nighttime scouting mission during the Battle of Chancellorsville)

43. Vicksburg, Mississippi

44. b.

45. d. (the U.S. Camel Corps, an experiment that faded with the coming of war)

46. c.

47. b.

48. Remington, born the year the Civil War began, contributed to *Harper's* years later

49. c. (Champion Hill, in Mississippi, was the site of another important battle, fought several weeks before the Battle of Gettysburg)

50. Andersonville, Georgia

51. Russia

52. c.

53. William C. Quantrill

54. a.

55. c.

56. The *Hunley*, an early submarine powered by an eight-man crew—seven to turn the hand-cranked prop and one to steer—rammed and sank a Union sloop; the *Hunley*, with its crew, sank too, but it was a first in submarine warfare

57. a.-i. (letter resigning his commission in the U.S. Army), b.-j. (telegram to Lincoln from Spotsylvania, on the way to Richmond), c.-f. (first message to the Confederate Congress), d.-g. (disregarding Rebel-mined waters in Mobile Bay), e.-h. (just before his March to the Sea, from Atlanta to Savannah)

58. a.-h. (after replacing Ambrose Burnside as commander of the Army of the Potomac), b.-j. (at Gettysburg), c.-i. (signaled across a valley to troops waiting for reinforcements at Allatoona Pass, Georgia), d.-f. (on watching the Battle of Fredericksburg), e.-g. (before being fatally shot at Spotsylvania, the line brilliantly edited by time into "They can't hit an elephant at this dist–")

59. e. (a line from Robert E. Lee, at the end of the war)

60. Major General Quincy Adams Gillmore (the limited-issue Gillmore Medal, today one of the rarest Civil War prizes)

61. a.-h., b.-j., c.-f., d.-g., e.-i. (extra points: Edward)

62. Cassius Marcellus Clay

63. b.

64. General Jubal Early (bonus: three days)

65. George ("Boo"), William ("Rooney"), and Robert E. Jr. ("Rob")

66. d.

67. The Battle of Cold Harbor, a failed assault on a Rebel stronghold that cost thousands of Union lives

68. George G. Meade

69. Judah P. Benjamin, C.S.A. secretary of war

70. Meade: Cádiz, Spain; Benjamin: St. Thomas, West Indies

71. a.

72. Hollywood honcho Irving Thalberg to Louis B. Mayer, speaking of an about-to-be-published novel by an unknown author named Margaret Mitchell (Mayer took a pass and David O. Selznick bought the rights and made a movie of which you may have heard: *Gone with the Wind*)

73. Salmon P. Chase was named Chief Justice of the United States (four years later, he presided over the impeachment trial of President Andrew Johnson)

74. Both were Union scouts

75. d. (bonus: Raphael Semmes captained the *Alabama*, John Winslow the *Kearsarge*)

76. Mobile Bay

77. a.

78. "Aura Lee"

79. c.

80. Galusha Pennypacker

81. c.

82. c.

83. Jeb Stuart

84. Union troops, two months after they had suffered a defeat at Chickamauga

85. "Who touches a hair of yon gray head
Dies like a dog! March on!" he said.

86. c.

87. e., c., a., b., d.

88. a.

89. c.

90. Major Anderson, who had taken the Stars & Stripes with him after surrendering the fort to General Beauregard, raised the flag again

91. Major Henry Rathbone and his fiancée, Clara Harris

92. c.

93. a.

94. Battle of Palmito Ranch

95. *Sultana*

96. a. *The Great Locomotive Chase*, b. *Friendly Persuasion*, c. *Band of Angels*, d. *Shenandoah*, e. *The Birth of a Nation*

97. Tennessee was first, on July 24, 1866; Georgia was last, on July 15, 1870

98. Katie

99. He was Lincoln's assigned bodyguard at Ford's Theatre, and he didn't stop John Wilkes Booth; whether he should have, or could have, and exactly what he was or wasn't doing at the historic moment, is, and probably always will be, up for grabs

100. a. The thirteenth, b. Illinois (February 1, 1865), c. Georgia (December 6, 1865), d. Mississippi (March 16, 1995), having rejected it 130 years earlier), e. Delaware and Kentucky